Freedom from Generational Sin

Ruth Hawkey

New Wine Press

New Wine Press
PO Box 17
Chichester
England PO19 2AW

All Scripture quotations are taken from the New King James Version,
copyright © 1983 by Thomas Nelson, Inc.

ISBN: 1 874367 88 4

Typeset by CRB Associates, Reepham, Norfolk.
Printed in Malta

Contents

Preface

Having taught into the subject of 'Generational Sin' for a number of years now, at various seminars around the country, I have found that it has often been received either with great delight or with the very relevant query, 'Is this scriptural?' I hope to show that it is both scriptural and very applicable to today's Christians. My desire is that the reader will begin to see answers to some of the questions which may have puzzled them for years.

Such questions for instance as, 'Why is it that I seem to be repeating the pattern of fears and phobias that obsessed my mother's life even though I have tried repeatedly to change?' Or 'Why do I find pornography books so difficult to lay down?' or 'What is the reason that I find the pornographic material on the Internet so difficult to resist? I have tried to withstand looking at it, I have fasted and prayed, I have cried out to God, but all to little or no effect. I am still hooked.'

Or the questioner may ask, 'Why am I so fascinated with the occult? My family are second generation Christians, so where does the strong interest spring from?' Or as one person said to me, 'My grandfather was an abuser, my father was an abuser, I have been an abuser. What can I do to stop my children from falling into the same trap?'

I hope to show that, whilst such folk have the responsibility of dealing with their own personal sin, nevertheless many of them may also be battling against the sins of their ancestors. It may be that they are inheriting the weaknesses of previous generations, and until those weaknesses are recognised, confessed and repented of, they will continue to struggle to walk into the freedom which Christ died to bring them.

This book is a response to those people who have heard the teaching on 'Generational Sin', and who have asked that the teaching be presented in written form for their future reference and help. My hope and prayer is that it will be a blessing to most people and a means of release to many in the Body of Christ.

Ruth Hawkey

Chapter 1

The Laws of God

Whoever we are, and wherever we have been born, whether it is in Britain, Jamaica, New Zealand or as far away as in the deepest forests of North Borneo, it is an undoubted truth that we are all born into a family. This lineage will have a certain amount of generational blessing as well as generational sin built into it. For none of us have come into this world born to completely innocent parents with an impeccable pedigree, and whilst it is true that some of us have inherited more good than evil, all of us to some extent, have to carry our generational baggage around with us!

Most of us carry a crate-load of mixed blessings and cursing, for it is a truism that in many cases it is a question of 'like mother, like daughter'! 'Like father, like son'! This is called the law of 'Generational Blessing, and Generational Iniquity' both of which we will look at in more detail in a moment.

There are a number of laws which are written into God's universe. These are decrees which God has intended to be used for our good, in order that we may be a blessed people who will live happy and fruitful lives. However, they are also laws which, if we withstand or disobey them, may also be used for our ill, especially if we do not fulfil their conditions. For example, one of the most important laws in God's universe is the **Law of Blessing and Curse**.

In Deuteronomy chapter 28, we are told all about God's promises of blessing if we obey His commandments. These blessings are many and bounteous and include fruitfulness, health and a long life. God intends that these blessings will pass down the family line, so that not only will **we** be blessed, but our children will be blessed also. He promises us that:

> *'The righteous man walks in his integrity;*
> *His children are blessed after him.'* (Proverbs 20:7)

People in the natural world, of course, are very aware of the good things which come down the family line, for they will often remark that 'Mary' is just like her grandpa, especially in the area of creativity, and that she also shows a remarkable likeness to her mother's sister. You will hear them comment on the fact that 'John' is just like his father, very musical and excellent on the piano. They will even note and remark on the truth, that 'Ruth' is just like her grandmother, delightful in nature, full of fun but with a strong and determined spirit! In fact they may even mention, that being a redhead like her great grandmother, she has also inherited that lady's fiery temper, as well as her warm and independent nature!

Christians are also very much aware of the blessings which are passed from one age to another; all of the good things, both material and spiritual, which are transferred down the generational line. For example, we can see the pattern of faith being passed down the family line in the life of Paul's companion Timothy. We are told that Timothy inherited his faith from his mother and his grandmother.

> *'I call to remembrance the genuine faith that is in you, which*
> *dwelt first in your grandmother Lois and your mother Eunice.'*
> (2 Timothy 1:5)

One can just imagine the godly grandmother of Timothy praying so much for her grandchild and being delighted to see the faithfulness of God, as He brings him to the place of like faith.

We also see the mercy of God coming down the generation line:

> *'Therefore know that the Lord your God, He is God, the faithful God who keeps covenant and mercy for a thousand generations with those who love Him and keep His commandments.'* (Deuteronomy 7:9)

As, of course, does God's righteousness:

> *'But the mercy of the Lord is from everlasting to everlasting*
> *On those who fear Him,*
> *And His righteousness to children's children,*
> *To such as keep His covenant*
> *And to those who remember His commandments to do*
> *them.'* (Psalm 103:17–18)

As well as the law of blessing there is also, written into God's universe, the **Law of Multiplication**. This is linked to the law of blessing, in that our God is a bountiful God, and He means those blessings to be multiplied from generation to generation. So He wrote into the universe His plan for the multiplication of good things. Referring to animals and birds He said:

> *'And God blessed them, saying, "Be fruitful and multiply, and fill the waters in the seas, and let birds multiply on the earth." '* (Genesis 1:22)

Whilst referring to mankind His word was:

> *'Then God blessed them, and God said to them, "Be fruitful and multiply; fill the earth and subdue it." '* (Genesis 1:28)

God's multiplication flows out of God's abundant heart, for He desires to bless and be a blessing to His people throughout the generations. Therefore we see that His plan of multiplication is intricately linked into His plan of blessing. Peter and Jude knew the truth of this as we hear them praying for fellow Christians:

> *'Grace and peace be multiplied to you.'* (2 Peter 1:2)

'Mercy, peace, and love be multiplied to you.'   (Jude 1:2)

The disciples are very much aware that the blessings of peace, grace, love and mercy are not to be given meagrely by God, but instead He will shower them down upon His people according to His law of multiplication.

However, the plans of God are also linked into another one of God's laws, which is called the **Law of Sowing and Reaping**. Scripture tells us that if we sow upright actions, good habits, righteous attitudes and principles into our family line, then God will cause us to reap those things a thousand fold, for the multiplication factor comes into effect again. Nevertheless, God's law of sowing and reaping also includes the element of **justice**, for it is based on the principle of 'whatsoever' we sow into our families (whether it is good or bad), that is what we will reap.

'Do not be deceived, God is not mocked; for whatsoever a man sows, that he will also reap.   (Galatians 6:7)

Sin always has its consequences, and if we are in any doubt about that, we only have to consider the experiences of the nation of Israel. Speaking to the Israelite people God says:

'Sow for yourselves righteousness;
Reap in mercy;
Break up your fallow ground,
For it is time to seek the Lord,
Till He comes and rains righteousness on you.
You have ploughed wickedness;
You have reaped iniquity.'   (Hosea 10:12–13)

Thus, as well as blessings, we see that sinful actions and thoughts can also pass down the family line. This of course, is a distortion of God's original intention of passing multiplied benefits from one generation to another. This may result in illness, curses. and mental and emotional disturbances repeating themselves constantly in the family structure. So the sowing may be either good or bad. It can be a present-day sowing or one that was sown way back in the generational line. The effects of sin may also be out of all proportion to the sowing; thus we see the multiplication factor coming into fulfilment again. Hosea 8:7 says:

'They sow the wind, and reap the whirlwind.'

There is an interesting story recorded in Judges chapter 1, concerning the war between Judah and Simeon, and the Canaanites. It tells the story of the king of that country, Adoni-Bezek, and relates how Judah and Simeon cut off his thumbs and big toes. Adoni-Bezek, in a moment of enlightenment recalls that:

'Seventy kings with their thumbs and big toes cut off used to gather their food under my table; as I have done, so God has repaid me.' (Judges 1:7)

This is a remarkable example of the law of sowing and reaping being at work within God's universe, for what Adoni-Bezek sowed, he also reaped. Here we find that he suffered the very same punishment as he had inflicted upon those seventy kings: his thumbs and toes were also truncated.

I am reminded of a lady I prayed for, who (to the surprise of both of us) was certainly carrying the grief from a great number of abortions, which had taken place in her generational line. The descendant was reaping the consequences of her parents' and her grandparents' sins.

Whilst the multiplication factor does come into effect in this law of sowing and reaping, nevertheless God in His mercy, has limited the consequences of the father's sins to three and four generations, whilst the law of blessing goes on for thousands!

'And the Lord passed before him and proclaimed, "The Lord, the Lord God, merciful and gracious, longsuffering, and abounding in goodness and truth, keeping mercy for thousands, forgiving iniquity and transgression and sin, by no means clearing the guilty; visiting the iniquity of the fathers

> *upon the children and the children's children to the third and
> the fourth generation.'* (Exodus 34:6–7)

The writer of Deuteronomy confirms the consequences of sin:

> *'Then the Lord will bring upon you and your descendants
> extraordinary plagues – great and prolonged plagues – and
> prolonged sicknesses.'* (Deuteronomy 28:59)

It is interesting to note that the writer reiterates that it is also the descendants who will suffer the consequences of the father's sin. Thus we find that the law of sowing and reaping, whilst linking in to the law of blessing, also links in with another law in God's universe, and that is the **Law of Generational Iniquity**.

The important question would seem to be, 'What do we mean by generational iniquity?' The word itself is used in a number of scriptures, and in the context of the Ten Commandments, as recorded in Exodus 20:5, we hear God saying:

> *'I, the Lord your God, am a jealous God, visiting the iniquity
> of the fathers on the children to the third and fourth
> generations of those who hate me.'*

What then does the word 'iniquity' mean? In order to consider the meaning of the word 'iniquity' it may help us to look at some of the other words, which are used for 'sin' within the Scriptures. The word **'sin'** (*hamartia*) occurs over two hundred and fifty times in the New Testament and has the root idea, of falling short; an error; a failure; an independence of God. The word **'transgression'** (*parabasis*) carries with it the meaning of the breaking of a specific rule or law. The word **'trespass'** (*paraptoma*) means going onto forbidden territory; going where you shouldn't in spite of warnings and notices.

The word **'iniquity'** (*avon*) is used in many passages in the Old Testament (including Exodus 20:5), and carries the meaning of 'perversity' and according to the New King James

Version the word 'iniquity' (*anomia*) as recorded in the New Testament, literally means 'lawlessness'. So the word has within it the idea of some sin or sins, resulting from a wrong desire, lawlessness, or a perverseness, which then causes a weakness and a compulsion in the make-up of our descendants or in us as a result of the sins of our ancestors.

The commentator C.J. Ellicott DD writes:

'All history shows that this is a law of God's moral government of the world.'

The fact is, that when our ancestors sin, there is the possibility of the consequence of their sin falling upon us. We are then vulnerable to sinning in the same areas and so compounding the problem for our children in the family line.

Exodus 20:5 says that if the people disobey the Ten Commandments (the Law) then the Lord will visit the iniquities of the fathers upon the children to the third and fourth generation. This results in a **flaw – a weakness, and a tendency to sin in that particular area by the family**. Like a **flaw** in a rock, so the initial sin introduces a tendency towards breaking the Law in the same area as the original sin. Leviticus chapter 26 hammers this message home:

'*And those of you who are left shall waste away in their iniquity in your enemies' lands; also in their fathers' iniquities, which are with them, they shall waste away.*'

(Leviticus 26:39)

Jeremiah, whom many people believe wrote the book of Lamentations, writes:

'*Our fathers sinned and are no more,*
But we bear their iniquities.'   (Lamentations 5:7)

And in case we are in any doubt, the writer of Deuteronomy says that the Lord will be:

'*. . . visiting the iniquity of the fathers upon the children to the third and fourth generation.*'   (Deuteronomy 5:9)

Jeremiah picks up the theme again in the book named after him and asserts that:

> *'You show lovingkindness to thousands, and repay the iniquity of the fathers into the bosom of their children after them.'* (Jeremiah 32:18)

Chapter 2

Some Common Objections to Generational Iniquity

What about the **sour grapes**?

> *'In those days they shall say no more:*
> *"The fathers have eaten sour grapes,*
> *And the children's teeth are set on edge."'*
>
> (Jeremiah 31:29)

Ezekiel, the prophet, quotes the same proverb as Jeremiah and some people might well legitimately ask the question, 'What about Ezekiel chapter 18 and Jeremiah chapter 31. Where do they fit in with the view of generational iniquity?' These chapters refer to the fact that each man shall bear the consequences of his **own** sin. According to the commentator C.J. Ellicott DD, these chapters were written in the context of judgement and he carefully points out that both of the prophets are keen to stress that there is, and must be, a place for individual responsibility.

Both Jeremiah and Ezekiel are writing to people who were inclined to blame their own sins on the sins of their fathers. They evaded their own personal responsibility, and so both of the prophets want to bring home to them the stark truth that God will judge each man for his own sin. People were finding in the words of Exodus 20:5 an excuse for their own personal sin, rather than seeing it as a warning against passing on the weakness to their children.

C.J. Ellicott DD emphasises that the law of generational iniquity leaves untouched the freedom of man's free will. In this context he writes:

> 'Thus it is true that God does both visit the sins of the fathers upon the children and at the same time does, through all, punish and reward each single person according to their own individual bearing towards Him.'

He also states:

> 'Individual suffering is certainly the consequence of individual sin ... but these consequences are often slow in their development and may not fall upon the individual who has done the wrong, but upon some more or less remote descendants.'

Thus we see that there is room in the Scriptures for both man's freedom of choice as to whether to sin or not, and also the fact that the sins of the fathers are visited upon the children to the third and fourth generation. One does not exclude the other; neither does one excuse the other, for both are valid.

Another common objection is the view that we are now under a **New Covenant** and therefore the Old Covenant is null and void. It is certainly true that we are under a New Covenant with the coming of the Lord Jesus Christ and His death upon the Cross. I hope to show in a later chapter the full benefits of the New Covenant, which Jesus has won for us. However, I would simply remind the reader that the New does not dispense with the Old, for as Jesus pointed out:

> *'Do not think that I came to destroy the Law or the Prophets. I did not come to destroy but to fulfill. For assuredly, I say to you, till heaven and earth pass away, one jot or one tittle will by no means pass from the law till all is fulfilled.'*
>
> (Matthew 5:17–18)

It is also very important for us to realise that just as we go to the Cross to appropriate for ourselves forgiveness for our own personal sin, so in a like manner we need to go to the

Cross to appropriate what Jesus has won for us, in the removal of our family sin. We need to walk in the full benefits of the New Covenant, rather than knowing freedom in part, whilst still carrying around the weakness of our family iniquity. If it is correct that:

'You shall know the truth, and the truth shall set you free,'
(John 8:32)

then the more knowledge we have of what is entailed in the New Covenant, the more possible it is to walk in the truth of it, and therefore claim the benefits entailed and walk in its blessing.

Another common objection might be, 'But it is so unfair, why should I suffer because of what some unknown ancestor did or did not do?' The observation is true, in that it is so obviously unfair, but once Adam and Eve had sinned, unfortunately they introduced unfairness into the system. The laws of God are neutral and are based on obedience and blessing, and the unfairness began because of man's sin. As we have seen already, the laws of God work for either good or ill, since these laws are just and unbiased. The wonder of it is, is that God in His mercy and through His Grace, found a way through the work of the Lord Jesus Christ, to redeem man and to provide the means for the iniquity to be stopped on the Cross.

Chapter 3

Biblical Evidence of Generational Iniquity – Sexual Sin

Two of the most basic questions would seem to be:
- 'Does Scripture bear out the evidence of generational iniquity?'
- 'Do the families, as depicted in the Bible, show that the pattern of sin; the breaking of God's law in a particular area; the tendency to sin in the same way, continues repeatedly down the family line?'

According to Exodus 20:14 the Lord commands us:

> *'You shall not commit adultery.'*

Usually, adultery is a description of a married person having sexual intercourse outside of marriage. However, in the margin of the Amplified Bible, adultery is described as sexual sin in the widest sense. The writer asserts:

> 'Observe here the expansion of the meaning of the seventh commandment in many catechisms to include whoredom in all its forms, as well as unchastity "premarital relations, sexual impurity, and lustful desire under whatever name." (J.P. Lange, *A Commentary*). "Not only is adultery forbidden here, but also fornication and all kinds of mental and sensual uncleanness. All impure books, songs, pictures etc., which tend to inflame and debauch the mind are against this law." (Adam Clarke, *The Holy Bible with a Commentary*)'

In the context of sexual sin it is interesting to observe how the pattern of immorality is repeated generation after generation in the family line of King David. He was a descendant of the line of Judah, who was the son of Jacob and Rachel. Judah had intercourse, inadvertently, with his daughter-in-law, Tamar. In Genesis chapter 38, we read the story of the incestuous relationship between them, and even though it was unintentional on Judah's part, nevertheless he introduced into his family line a tendency to sin in this particular way. According to Deuteronomy chapter 27 there is a curse which will come upon those who commit incest and this curse will pass down the family line. Leviticus, chapter 18 also warns against sexual sin and its consequences and in verse 15 we read:

> *'You shall not uncover the nakedness of your daughter-in-law – she is your son's wife – you shall not uncover her nakedness.'*

Judah, through his intercourse with Tamar, exposed her nakedness and the fruit of their union were twin boys, Zerah and Perez. As we consider the family line of Perez we see that the same weakness, the same flaw, the same tendency to sin in the sexual area is passed down the generational line.

There were ten generations between Judah and King David, the book of Ruth 4:18–22 gives the genealogy of Perez's family line. God normally restricted the sins of the fathers to three or four generations, but for sexual sin we read in Deuteronomy chapter 23 that it was to be for ten generations.

> *'One of illegitimate birth shall not enter the congregation of the Lord; even to the tenth generation none of his descendants shall enter the congregation of the Lord.'*

(Deuteronomy 23:2)

It is very interesting to note that King David's son, Amnon, also has an incestuous relationship with his half-sister, who is also called Tamar. In the King James Version of the Bible, 2 Samuel chapter 13 is entitled 'Incest in David's House', but in actuality the incest had been in his house from the original sin of Judah and his daughter-in-law Tamar. In a very real sense, whilst King David and his son Amnon were very much responsible for their own sins they were also walking in the sins of their fathers.

In this sphere of sexual sin, we can also see the sin of abuse within marriage being passed down the family line. Three generations of Abraham's family abuse their relationship with their wives, Abraham being the one to introduce the weakness, and the flaw into the line.

Abraham Opens Sarah up to Possible Abuse

In Genesis 12:10–20 we have the story of Abraham travelling south because of a famine in the land in which they were living. As they approach Egypt, Abraham says to Sarah:

> *'Indeed I know that you are a woman of beautiful countenance. Therefore it will happen, when the Egyptians see you, that they will say, "This is his wife"; and they will kill me, but they will let you live. Please say that you are my sister, that it may be well with me for your sake, and that I may live because of you.'* (Genesis 12:11–13)

Abraham's abuse of Sarah lay in the fact that he removed his protection from her and opened her up to the possibility of committing sexual sin outside of her marriage.

God judged the situation very severely and sent plagues upon the house of Pharaoh. However, in Genesis chapter 20, we see Abraham repeating his sin, but this time he doesn't ask Sarah to lie for him, instead he lies himself:

> *'"She is my sister." And Abimelech king of Gerar sent and took Sarah.'* (Genesis 20:2)

Abraham was playing on the fact that she was indeed his half-sister, but we see that again he was opening his wife up to possible abuse. God judged that sin also, and in His mercy He protected both Sarah and Abraham by warning Abimelech in a dream and saying to him:

> *'Indeed you are a dead man because of the woman whom you have taken, for she is a man's wife.'*   (Genesis 20:3)

And God again closed the wombs of the women in his house. It is interesting to see that He allowed Abraham to pray for healing for the women and God heard his prayer,

> *'...and God healed Abimelech, his wife, and his maidservants. Then they bore children.'*   (Genesis 20:17)

Isaac Opens Rebekah up to Possible Abuse

The consequence of Abraham's sin was that the tendency to sin in the same area – the 'flaw', the iniquity – was passed onto his son Isaac:

> *'So Isaac dwelt in Gerar. And the men of the place asked him about his wife. And he said, "She is my sister"; for he was afraid to say, "She is my wife," because he thought, "lest the men of the place should kill me for Rebekah, because she is beautiful to behold."'*   (Genesis 26:6–7)

Just like his father, Isaac opened his wife, Rebekah, up to possible abuse, for we see here that Isaac repeats his father's sin! The consequence of Isaac's sin and the iniquity – the 'flaw', the weakness – was passed on to his son Jacob.

Jacob Opens Leah up to Possible Abuse

Jacob repeats his father's and his grandfather's sin but in a different way. The tendency – the flaw – comes out in a slightly altered manner, but nevertheless we can see his abuse of his wife, Leah. Jacob had been deceived by Laban and had been given Leah as his wife instead of Rachel her sister, whom he loved. He did not love Leah, at least in the beginning, and yet he had continual sexual intercourse with her. The names of her children give a vivid description of how Leah must have felt.

> *'When the Lord saw that Leah was unloved, He opened her womb; but Rachel was barren. So Leah conceived and bore a son, and she called his name Reuban; for she said, "The Lord has surely looked on my affliction. Now therefore, my husband will love me." '*
>
> (Genesis 29:31–32)

The word 'unloved' is literally translated 'hated'. Imagine having a sexual relationship with someone who hates you! The names of each of the children who followed spoke of Leah's abuse and misery. Her second son she called, Simeon, meaning:

> *'Because the Lord has heard that I am unloved.'*
>
> (Genesis 29:33)

Her third son she named Levi:

> *'Now this time my husband will become attached to me, because I have borne him three sons.'* (Genesis 29:34)

She is desperately trying to buy her husband's affection and protection. Leah goes on to have another child whom she names Judah, because she affirms *'Now I will praise the Lord.'* One feels that Leah has won through to a place of contentment and peace, with or without her husband's help. Jacob's sin was that he had sexual relationships with his wife whilst hatred was filling his heart. He used her for his own ends. He was repeating his father's and his grandfather's sin! We note here that indeed the sins of the fathers are visited upon the children, to the third and fourth generation, and to ten generations for sexual sin.

In the same family we see another weakness being passed down the family line, which, whilst it is not the same sin, is connected with it: that of dishonouring and deception. For linked into Abraham, Isaac and Jacob's abuse of their wives there was a strong thread of not honouring the wives whom God had given to them and also the willingness to deceive other people.

Chapter 4

Biblical Evidence of Generational Iniquity – Dishonouring and Deception

Jacob Dishonours and Deceives Isaac

In Exodus 20:12 God commands that people should:

'Honour your father and your mother that your days may be long upon the land.'

In Genesis chapter 27, we see Jacob being willing to dishonour and deceive his father Isaac, at his mother's instigation, by pretending to be Esau, and receive the blessing as the first-born. Esau, of course, when he finds out is devastated, as also is Isaac, his father, for we hear him crying out:

'Your brother came with deceit and has taken away your blessing.' (Genesis 27:35)

At that moment, a dishonouring of parents and a disposition to deception entered the family line. The weakness and the flaw were to continue for a number of generations.

It is very interesting to see that Jacob deceived and dishonoured his father (with his mother's help) by the use of two young goats. They killed them and used their skin for the clothing of Jacob's arms. Rebekah was totally involved in the deception:

> *'And she put the skins of the kids of the goats on his hands and on the smooth part of his neck.'*   (Genesis 27:16)

Jacob's Sons Deceive Him

It is enlightening to see the way in which Jacob's sons inherit and pass on their father's sin. For they too, in turn, dishonour and deceive him! The sin, iniquity, and weakness are passed on. It is interesting too, to see that they also use a goatskin in their deception! The brothers of Joseph, Jacob's favourite son, sell Joseph to the Ishmaelites, because they are jealous of the attention which he continually receives from their father. They dishonour their father by being willing to deceive him and in order to do this we read:

> *'So they took Joseph's tunic, killed a kid of the goats, and dipped the tunic in the blood. Then they sent the tunic of many colours, and they brought it to their father and said, "We have found this. Do you know whether it is your son's tunic or not?"'*   (Genesis 37:31–32)

They, too, make use of a kid of a goat.

Ham Dishonours His Father

There is an interesting story in Genesis chapter 9, concerning the family of Noah and his son Ham who dishonours his father through sexual perversion. One evening Noah got drunk and lay naked in his tent. Ham looked into the tent and saw his father's nakedness. On doing so he should have covered his father over and closed the opening of the tent to protect his father's honour, but instead he called out to his brothers Shem and Japheth to 'come and have a look.' Thus he dishonoured his father, for it was strictly forbidden:

> *'None of you shall approach anyone who is near of kin to him, to uncover his nakedness.'*   (Leviticus 18:6)

Shem and Japheth were more honouring of their father, for they went in backward and covered Noah up.

Ham's Sexual Sin Grows and Expands

However, in Ham's family line the sin, the iniquity, the weakness is passed on, for we see that Ham's descendants followed in their father's footsteps! When God was bringing the children of Israel into the land of Canaan (the descendants of Ham) He gave them strict instructions not to behave as the Canaanites do, for He says:

'I visit the punishment of its iniquity upon it.'

(Leviticus 18:25)

The warning, which He gives to the children of Israel, is in the whole context of sexual sin and sexual perversion. The original sin of Ham was that he dishonoured his father through his sexual depravity of looking on his father's nakedness. Thus his voyeurism introduced a weakness, a flaw, a tendency into his generational line, which multiplied and expanded in his descendants, so that eventually it included bestiality, homosexuality and incest as well. Truly it could be said of Ham and his descendants:

'The land is defiled.'   (Leviticus 18:25)

It is sobering to think that so much sin sprang from one man sinning and thus he introduced the weakness into his family line.

Chapter 5

Biblical Evidence of Generational Iniquity – Murder in the Family Line

In the context of the Ten Commandments, and therefore in the context of generational iniquity, the law states:

> *'You shall not commit murder.'* (Exodus 20:13)

Cain and Lamech

Looking at the family line of Cain, who murdered his brother Abel, we see that having introduced violence into his family line, his descendants suffer the consequences of his sin. His generational descendants are described in Genesis 4:16–24. One of Cain's descendants, Lamech, writes,

> *'For I have killed a man for wounding me,*
> *Even a young man for hurting me.*
> *If Cain shall be avenged sevenfold,*
> *Then Lamech seventy-sevenfold.'* (Genesis 4:23–24)

When God warned Cain, before he murdered his brother that:

> *'...sin lies at the door. And its desire is for you, but you should rule over it,'* (Genesis 4:7)

one gets the feeling that when Cain sinned he opened a generational door of murder and violence that continued to affect his generational line for many years. The iniquity, the 'flaw', in this instance, as with the sexual perversion of Ham, has passed down the line and grown in intensity, and we see Lamech almost boasting of his violent behaviour.

Esau and Jacob

In this area of murder and violence we can see the patterns of sin being repeated in the life of Esau and Jacob. We have already noted that Jacob stole Esau's blessing, and as a result hatred grew in Esau's heart.

> *'So Esau hated Jacob because of the blessing with which his father blessed him, and Esau said in his heart, "The days of mourning for my father are at hand; then I will kill my brother Jacob."'* (Genesis 27:41)

Here began a feud that was to cost countless lives throughout the history of the Israelite people, for Esau's descendants did much killing and were known as a very violent and vindictive people. Indeed his family, the Edomites, became known throughout the nation as a vengeful and warlike people. Ezekiel chapter 25 talks of the Edomites as being a very revengeful people and in Ezekiel chapter 35, God gave a description of their end. Speaking judgement on them He says:

> *'"Because you have had an ancient hatred, and have shed the blood of the children of Israel by the power of the sword at the time of their calamity, when their iniquity came to an end, therefore, as I live," says the Lord God, "I will prepare you for blood, and blood shall pursue you."'* (Ezekiel 35:5–6)

This was a horrifying judgement to descend upon Esau's family line, all springing from Esau's hatred in his heart for his brother Jacob. It is interesting to note that Esau did not kill his brother, but nevertheless he had determined to do so in his heart. It reminds us of the words of Jesus:

'You have heard that it was said to those of old, "You shall not murder," and whoever murders will be in danger of the judgement. But I say to you that whoever is angry with his brother shall be in danger of the judgement.'

(Matthew 5:21–22)

Murder of the Gibeonites

In this sphere of generational iniquity there is a very interesting story recorded in 2 Samuel chapter 21. Way back in Israel's history, Joshua had made a covenant with the Gibeonites. They had deceived him, by pretending to be from a far country and from a destitute people (Joshua 9). Joshua and the leadership had neglected to take counsel of the Lord and thus made a covenant with the Gibeonites, which had they sought the Lord, they could have been saved from. Nevertheless, Joshua was a man of his word and he had made a promise before God that he would care for them and protect them and to the best of his knowledge he did just that.

However, in King David's time there was a famine in the land, and David inquired of the Lord as to why this was so?

'And the Lord answered, "It is because of Saul and his bloodthirsty house, because he killed the Gibeonites."'

(2 Samuel 21:1)

God had brought judgement on the land of Israel because Saul had not kept the covenant which Joshua had made with the Gibeonites, but instead had slain them. King David went to the Gibeonites and asked them what they wanted?

'"Let seven men of his descendants be delivered to us, and we will hang them before the Lord in Gibeah of Saul, whom the Lord chose." And the king said, "I will give them."'

(2 Samuel 21:6)

Seven of Saul's descendants died in payment for Saul's sin, surely an instance of the children suffering for the sins of their fathers. It was only after the debt was paid that the famine was lifted.

'And after that God heeded the prayer for the land.'
(2 Samuel 21:14)

Jesus' Strong Words

In Matthew 23:29–32, Jesus makes some very interesting comments in this whole area of generational iniquity. He makes reference to the fact that the scribes and Pharisees are the:

'... sons of those who murdered the prophets.'
(Matthew 23:31)

He is referring to the murder of the prophets and the servants of God throughout Jewish history. He asserts that the scribes and Pharisees are tainted with their murder:

*'That on you may come all the righteous blood shed on the earth, from the blood of righteous Abel to the blood of Zechariah, son of Berechiah, whom **you murdered** between the temple and the altar.'* (Matthew 23:35)

The reference *'Abel to ... Zechariah'* would indicate to the Jewish people that Jesus was including the whole of the Scriptures. This accusation *'whom you murdered'* can only be understood in the light of generational iniquity. For these scribes and Pharisees were not actually alive at the time of the murders, although they were showing all the signs that they carried the flaw, the weaknesses of their fathers.

Chapter 6

Biblical Evidence of Generational Iniquity – Idolatry in the Family Line

According to Exodus 20:4–5 we are expressly forbidden to worship idols, and it is in especial reference to this that the Lord talks about visiting the sins of the fathers upon the children.

> *'You shall not make for yourself any carved image, or any likeness of anything that is in heaven above, or that is in the earth beneath, or that is in the water under the earth; you shall not bow down to them nor serve them. For I, the Lord your God am a jealous God, visiting the iniquity of the fathers on the children to the third and fourth generations of those who hate me.'*
> (Exodus 20:4–5)

In the worship of Molech, as referred to in Leviticus 20:1–5, God says that not only will He punish those who worship idols, He will also bring punishment upon those who compromise with the false worshipper. So serious is the sin of idol worship.

> *'And if the people of the land should in any way hide their eyes from the man, when he gives some of his descendants to Molech, and they do not kill him, then I will set my face against that man and against his family.'*
>
> (Leviticus 20:4–5)

False worship is like a root, which if left undealt with, will grow and spread into a bitter and poisonous plant.

> *'So that there may not be among you man or woman or family or tribe, whose heart turns away today from the Lord our God, to go and serve the gods of these nations, and that there may not be among you a root bearing bitterness or wormwood.'* (Deuteronomy 29:18)

Idolatry had the serious potential of spreading throughout the generations like a canker, which is why God spoke to strongly against it, and the history of Israel proves the great dangers inherent in it. The family of Israel's kings is an amazing illustration of a family who turned towards the worship of idols and thus brought upon themselves the words of Exodus 20:4–5.

There are some very interesting people in the family line of King David and his son, King Solomon. It is salutary that it was King Solomon himself who introduced idolatry into the family line:

> *'For it was so, when Solomon was old, that his wives turned his heart after other gods; and his heart was not loyal to the Lord his God, as was the heart of his father David.'*
>
> (1 Kings 11:4)

After Solomon's death the kingdom was divided into two: Israel and Judah, which was due to the foolishness of his son Rehoboam (1 Kings 12). All of the kings of Israel *'did evil in the sight of the Lord'* (1 Kings 15:34), and eventually they were taken into captivity. King Ahab was part of this line, as was his father Omri who

> *'... did evil in the eyes of the Lord, and did worse than all who were before him.'* (1 Kings 16:25)

However, because the line of Judah is the family line of Jesus we will consider and concentrate on those kings and their generational line. Reading the history of Judah, you will notice that every now and again there is a good king who tries to re-establish the worship of Jehovah. Nevertheless, mixed in with them, there often arises a king who continues to practise idolatry as Solomon did, when he took foreign wives and took their idolatry on board at the same time, introducing it into the family line.

The history as recorded in 1 Kings 14–23, makes very interesting reading as regards the teaching of generational iniquity and how the Lord continues to keep someone on the throne with the same heart as King David. The following kings were such men: Asa, Jehoshaphat, Hezekiah and Josiah. It was often written concerning them that:

> '... he did what was right in the sight of the Lord, according to all that his father David had done.'   (2 Kings 18:3)

In this instance the writer was referring to King Hezekiah, truly a man like King David, for he was a man after God's own heart. It is interesting however to see how the weakness and the flaw keeps resurrecting itself within the family, for Hezekiah's son, Manasseh, was the exact opposite of his father. He introduced terrible and wicked practices (as recorded in 2 Kings chapter 21) amongst the people of Judah.

In this area of idolatry, there is also included the sin of worshipping false religions as well as dabbling in any forbidden occult activity. King Manasseh was involved in all of these things. He raised up altars to Baal, he worshipped Assyrian gods, and he profaned the house of the Lord by building altars to false gods within them.

> 'Also he made his son pass through the fire, practised soothsaying, used witchcraft, and consulted spiritists and mediums. He did much evil in the sight of the Lord, to provoke Him to anger.'   (2 Kings 21:6)

Such things would bring the curse of God both upon the person involved, and on his family also, as we will see in the next chapter.

Chapter 7

The Power of the Curse

In the first chapter, I made reference to the law of 'blessing and curse' as recorded in Deuteronomy chapter 28, and how God's intention was that those blessings would pass down the family line. These would be given in response to people being obedient to God's laws. In the same chapter we have reference to what happens if we disobey His commandments and the terrible consequence of curse which will follow:

> *'But it shall come to pass, if you do not obey the voice of the Lord your God, to observe carefully all His commandments and His statutes which I command you today, that all these curses will come upon you and overtake you.'*
>
> (Deuteronomy 28:15)

We need to always remember that the reason why God places a curse, is in order to bring a person or a family under judgement and therefore to a place where they can receive His mercy and forgiveness. This, hopefully, will eventually lead them to confession, repentance, forgiveness and freedom.

Having ascertained God's purposes in bringing a curse upon a person, let us look at a few of the specific curses, as recorded in Deuteronomy chapter 27; looking at what they are, how they are given; and in what way they work within the family line.

Curses Passed Down the Line

As we have seen, the main reason for God's curse falling upon a person and his family is in response to their disobedience and the breaking of His laws, that is the Ten Commandments.

> *'And they* [the curses] *shall be upon you for a sign and a wonder, and on your descendants forever.'*
>
> (Deuteronomy 28:46)

False Religions, Occult, Idolatry, Worship of Other Gods

As we have seen, any worship of foreign gods invokes the wrath of the true and living God.

> *'Cursed is the one who makes any carved or moulded image, an abomination to the Lord.'* (Deuteronomy 27:15)

This false worship would include being involved with any religion that denies the humanity and the divinity of the Lord Jesus Christ: for example, Jehovah's Witnesses, Freemasonry, Spiritualism, Christian Science, etc.,

Dishonouring of Parents

To dishonour parents is a very serious sin in the eyes of the Lord, for they are the ones who are intended to input the true 'fear of the Lord' into the child and to 'raise him up in the way in which he should go.' Therefore God speaks a curse on anyone who dishonours his or her mother and father.

> *'Cursed is the one who treats his father or mother with contempt.'* (Deuteronomy 27:16)

Injustice and Oppression

Injustice and oppression is a great abomination to the Lord, for His heart is for the underdog, for those who have no one to stand up for their cause. He especially has a heart for the weak or the helpless and God is very much against the man or woman who rides upon their backs for their own advancement. Deuteronomy 27:17–19 talk about the various unjust situations which will bring God's curse upon a person and his descendants. These include the orphan, the foreigner and the woman without a husband:

> *'Cursed is the one who perverts the justice due the stranger, the fatherless, and the widow.'*   (Deuteronomy 27:19)

Sexual Sin

As we have seen, any sexual sin brings consequences upon the family line, but here in Deuteronomy we are told that it actually also brings a curse upon the person and the family.

> *'Cursed is the one who lies with his father's wife.'*
> (Deuteronomy 27:20)

> *'Cursed is the one who lies with any kind of animal.'*
> (Deuteronomy 27:21)

> *'Cursed is the one who lies with his sister.'*
> (Deuteronomy 27:22)

> *'Cursed is the one who lies with his mother-in-law.'*
> (Deuteronomy 27:23)

Here we see that bestiality, incest, and sexual perversion all bring a curse upon the person and his generational line.

Stealing and Lying

In this area of curse, there are some very interesting verses in Zechariah 5:1–4. Referring to thieves and robbers God says:

> *' "I will send out the curse," says the Lord of hosts;*
> *"It shall enter the house of the thief*
> *And the house of the one who swears falsely by My name.*

*It shall remain in the midst of his house
And consume it, with its timber and stones." '*

(Zechariah 5:4)

The word 'house' in Hebrew really means, 'the family, the structure', and in fact everything concerned with the person. There have been a number of times when we have prayed with people around their houses because they have sensed that there may be a curse at work. As they have confessed and repented of anything ungodly which may have gone on in the past, so there has come a lightening and a cleansing of the atmosphere within the house.

The Curse of Words

As well as God, a person can also put a curse upon another, and in this area words are very powerful indeed. Especially powerful are the words of any authority figures, for example the words of a **spouse** can go very deep, and in this context I find the words of Jacob to his wife Rachel very interesting. Rachel stole some family idols from her father's house; this was a sin in itself, of course, and a sin that would have brought a curse upon her and her descendants. When her father, Laban, is searching for the family idols, Jacob virtually curses his wife with the words:

' "With whomever you find your gods, do not let him live. In the presence of our brethren, identify what I have of yours and take it with you." For Jacob did not know that Rachel had stolen them.' (Genesis 31:32)

It is informative that Rachel had already brought herself under God's curse by worshipping false images. It is also interesting that in order to hide the idols, she proceeded to sit upon them. The place where she hid the false gods, became the place of her death, for it was as she brought forth her child from her womb, past the place where she had put the idols, that Rachel died. She either had, or pretended to have, her monthly period, therefore there would appear to be a direct connection between the hiding of the false gods and the means of her death. There is a real power in the curse of words: 'Do not let him live,' says Jacob, probably never even realising that he was talking about Rachel, his wife.

Parents

A parent's words to a child are also very forceful as well as powerful and they can keep the children under a curse for months or even years, for it is very true that:

> 'Death and life are in the power of the tongue.'
>
> > (Proverbs 18:21)

A baby can even hear the blessing or cursing of the words of his parents, as early as in the first few months whilst he or she is being formed within the womb. Luke 1:41 affirms that it was whilst John the Baptist was in the womb, that he responded to the words of Mary the mother of Jesus:

> '. . . when Elizabeth heard the greeting of Mary, that the babe leaped in her womb.'

Therefore if a baby hears such words of cursing as: 'I hate this baby, it will never amount to anything;' 'I don't want this child;' 'I am going to get rid of this baby;' then that curse of words can have a long and a lasting effect. Until a certain age, parents are as God to a child and if our mothers or fathers have said to us in the past, 'You're useless,' 'You're hopeless,' 'You're no good,' 'You're pathetic,' 'Nobody will ever want to marry you,' then we probably will believe them. The words will go straight into our spirit and we may begin to live according to their expectation of us, and according to the curse which they have placed upon us.

If a parent has been exceedingly strict with a child, then their very strictness may put fear into them and this will be as an entrance door, which will allow their words to become like arrows penetrating their spirit and causing them to walk under the curse. One lady was labouring under the curse of her father, who happened to be a sergeant major both on the parade ground and at home. His voice held such power and authority over her that whatever he said, 'must be true.' His words were, 'You are a disgrace to this family and you will be a shame to any other family which you might become a part of.' She married in her early twenties, and for years lived under the curse of those words. Her husband was never able to understand why she continually apologised for both herself and their children.

Teachers

In this domain of curse of words, teachers are very important to the young child, for they take over the parent's authority to some extent. Their words can be for good or ill, and many a child will believe that if the teacher says it, then it must be true! I am reminded of the teacher who literally dragged a child out to the front of the class and made fun of him because he didn't know his ten-times table. She was hoping to make an example of him, so that the other children would do their homework that night and pass their test the following morning. However, the words she used rang in that boy's ears until he was a grown man of thirty. 'You are stupid, you'll never make anything of yourself.' He was a bright boy, but he never did amount to anything – intellectually. He believed the teacher's pronouncements!

Church Leaders

The words of other authoritarian people are also very power-ful and some leaders have abused their position and spoken words which have set people back for years in the Christian life, as have also the words of some **threatening figures**. A prime example would be that of **Jezebel** and her curse of words upon Elijah. After Elijah had called upon God on Mount Carmel to answer by fire, and had killed the prophets of Baal, Jezebel comes and threatens to take his life.

> *'And Ahab told Jezebel all that Elijah had done, also how he had executed all the prophets with the sword. Then Jezebel sent a messenger to Elijah, saying, "So let the gods do to me,*

and more also, if I do not make your life as the life of one of them by tomorrow about this time." '   (1 Kings 19:1–2)

Those words were enough to send Elijah into a spiral of despair, for they went straight into his spirit and totally crushed him. I believe that was why he ran off into the wilderness. Words are very powerful and they can crush, bruise and break the spirit, which is why the writer of Proverbs affirms that:

'Death and life are in are power of the tongue.'
(Proverbs 18:21)

Abuser

Another threatening situation may be that of abuse, for abusers will very often put a curse of words upon a person whom they have abused, in order to keep them silent. This happened to Jane, a little girl who was bound into secrecy by her abuser for, 'If you tell your mother she will be sent to prison.' So strong was the curse of words, that even when she grew into womanhood, she found it impossible to share the deepest secrets of her heart with her husband and her family. However, not only did she suffer but also the whole family came under a cloud of secrecy. It is interesting to observe that James writes that,

' . . . the tongue is a fire, a world of iniquity. The tongue is so set among our members that it defiles the whole body, and sets on fire the course of nature; and it is set on fire by hell.'
(James 3:6)

Certainly in Jane's situation, her whole family was defiled and suffered the consequences of the abuser's sin. It is also possible of course, for a curse to be put upon a person from a number of other sources, which it is not in the remit of this book to consider, as we are simply looking at family weaknesses and curses as a result of family sin. However, there are some excellent books on the market, which give a fuller description of curses and their results.

Chapter 8

Indications of a Curse at Work

There will be several indications if a curse is at work within a person's life or within a family, one of which may be that **repeated sicknesses** can develop in the family line. In regards to the curses which will come on people for disobedience, Deuteronomy 28:59 affirms:

> *'then the Lord will bring upon you and your descendants extraordinary plagues – great and prolonged plagues – and serious and prolonged sicknesses.'*

Some people's families struggle with continued infirmity; backaches, migraines, stomach trouble, etc., which may spring from many and varied sources. They could be purely physical or emotional in nature, but they also could be as a result of a curse at work within the family.

An illustration of such a curse is to be found in the very interesting story of Elisha and his servant Gehazi. In 2 Kings chapter 5 we have the incident which is recorded, of the time when God healed Naaman, a commander of the army of the King of Syria, of leprosy. Naaman had been so delighted with his healing, that as a token of thanks he had offered Elisha a gift, but Elisha had refused it because Naaman's healing was the work of God. Gehazi, Elisha's servant, did not have similar principles and so he goes after Naaman and tells him that Elisha has changed his mind. He then takes from Naaman some silver. When he returns to Elisha, he receives a rebuke from Elisha and these words:

> ' "*Therefore the leprosy of Naaman shall cling to you and your descendants forever.*" *And he went out from his presence leprous, as white as snow.*'
> (2 Kings 5:27)

Gehazi's generational line suffered the consequences of Gehazi's sin.

Another clue that a curse may be at work within a family is if there is a pattern of frequent **marriage breakdown** within the generations. Maybe you see a pattern of divorce, separation, or family discord in the generational line. We have prayed into a number of marriages which had a curse put on them by one of the sets of parents, even before the couple arrived at the altar! 'This marriage will never work.' 'You are totally incompatible,' or as one father said to his daughter, 'There will always be your room ready, when you decide you have had enough.' It has been said that persistent opposition by parents to a marriage is closely linked with marital breakdown, although the writer could not understand the mechanism which was at work. He was not a Christian. One would wonder if this were an example of a curse of words being at work.

An atmosphere of **poverty**, if it were frequently repeated, would appear to be a sign of a curse at work, and would always be worth exploring as a possible cause. We have prayed with a number of people who have had ancestors who have been freemasons, only to find that repeated infirmity or poverty has been a result within the person or their descendants when they have left the lodge. The writer of Deuteronomy says:

> '*Cursed shall be your basket and your kneading bowl. Cursed shall be the fruit of your body and the produce of your land, the increase of your cattle and the offspring of your flocks.*'
> (Deuteronomy 28:17–18)

A very descriptive picture of abject poverty, which you will notice, can also include the state of childlessness, although this is not necessarily the only reason for this condition.

A **proneness to accidents** may also indicate that there is a curse at work, linked in with a pattern of **early** or **untimely deaths**. One man, for whom we prayed, was ill with a kidney problem. His father had died at approximately the same age as our friend, which was in his early forties. Not only that, but his grandfather also died at the same age. It was almost too much of a coincidence. One man who was approaching his fifties said, 'Something overtook my father's father when he was in his fifties, I am in my fifties, I feel rocked by waves of hundreds of years.' He had a nervous breakdown shortly afterwards.

Of course, we need to remember that the reason why God places a curse upon a person, is in response to that person's sin and disobedience and it is there in order to bring that person or family under judgement. This will hopefully lead to their confession and repentance, as well as direct them towards forgiveness and freedom.

The way to deliverance from a curse is very similar to the way in which we would bring a person to freedom in any other area. First of all there needs to be a **confession** of faith in Jesus as the deliverer and the one who carried our curse for us on the Cross. Secondly, there needs to be **confession and repentance** for any sin in our own lives, or in the life of our ancestors, which has allowed the curse to find a landing place. We may know what that is, or we may simply need to take accountability for any family sin which has brought the curse into effect.

There will need to be **forgiveness** of the family for any sin which they have committed, and which has brought the consequences of the curse onto the family. The person for whom you are praying, will need to **renounce** all contact with the occult, false worship etc., depending on the reason for the curse coming into being, if this is known. The **prayer of release** is also vital, and a suggested prayer might be:

'Thank you Jesus for dying on the Cross to take my curse upon Yourself. I ask You now to release me from every curse that has been operating in my life because of my own, or my family's sin. By faith I receive that release and thank You for it in Jesus Name.'

Chapter 9

Modern Examples of Sin Travelling Down the Family Line

We have seen how generational iniquity travels down the family line within the families in Scripture, but the question now would seem to be: 'Is there similar evidence that the same sin or weakness happens today?' A social worker that was sitting in on a teaching course which we were holding, confirmed to us that in the secular world they know all about generational iniquity. For him there was little doubt, for to them it is a fact of life that abuse, alcoholism, adultery, etc., often, although not inevitably, will run in families.

Sexual Sin

As we were teaching on this subject, a man who was at the seminar suddenly realised that he, his father, his grandfather and now his sons had all been involved with **molesting** young boys. Surprisingly, this gave him a great deal of hope, rather than adding to his despair, for he began to see a reason for his sin and for the family weakness which was so evident within himself and his sons. He also began to see the possibility of the sin and the iniquity, being dealt with at the Cross.

Another man, with whom we prayed, had begun **abusing** girls when he was eleven years old. (The girl had approached him for a sexual relationship; she was around the age of twelve to thirteen at the time.) By the age of eighteen he had committed **incest** with his mother, and in his early twenties he had found out, to his great surprise and shame, that he was simply following in his father's footsteps. The pattern of his sin was almost an identical copy of his father's, who had also experienced intercourse with his own mother and had also indulged in a lifetime of affairs.

Mary was six years old when her uncle first began to abuse her, and for years she shared her guilty secret with no one. However, on sharing about the abuse with her mother much later in life, she was amazed to learn that not only had her mum been abused around the age of six, but so also had her maternal grandmother! Three generations of abuse, beginning at the same age – surely it was too much of a coincidence.

Alcohol and Adultery

Alcohol and adultery are fairly well-known patterns of behaviour, which can be observed as repeating patterns within families. Dr Bonnie Eaker Weil did some research into the subject of adultery, and affirms that she now believes that infidelity can be inherited. She also believes that knowledge of these patterns of adultery in a person's past can help the present-day couple avoid a break up. Writing in the *Daily Express* on Tuesday, 3 August, 1993 she says,

> 'At that moment I began to see that adultery – much like alcoholism or abuse – was a multi-generational thing.'

She goes on,

> 'I've counselled more than 1,000 couples, 80 per cent because one or the other had been unfaithful. In nine out of ten cases, sometimes involving four generations

with grandparents as well as parents and children, at least one partner was the adult child of an adulterer.'

The same pattern can often be seen in the alcoholic and his descendants. We have observed a number of men, whose father and grandfather and now their sons have all walked the same path of being unable to resist drinking to excess. It is often when parents see the patterns being repeated in their children that they begin to look at their family line and yearn for release from the weakness and the flaw, which is not only blighting them but is now beginning to blight their children as well. The same pattern of family sin is, of course, sometimes seen in the drug abuser and his family.

Dishonouring Parents

Dishonouring parents can sometimes be seen travelling down the generational line as well. Maybe the parents will notice that there is an attitude of rebellion amongst their children, a putting down of the parents in front of others; in fact, they and others may remark that within the young people there is a standing against any authority and parental figures. This rebellion is usually in spite of there being some good and genuine discipline within the home.

Murder, Rage and Anger

Murder, rage and anger can also keep appearing within the family line. A man spoke to us fairly recently because he was troubled with outbursts of deep anger towards others who seemed to be a threat to him. This was eventually traced to his ancestry, which were the Scottish clans to which he belonged. His father, his grandfather and his great grandfather had all struggled with outbursts of rage. It was revealed, through his own research into the family history, that his great, great grandfather had murdered someone in one of the raids upon the English.

Stealing

Sometimes you will notice a tendency to steal or pilfer within a family – a tendency to take what is not yours. I am reminded of the story of Achan, as recorded in Scripture in the book of Joshua, chapter 7. Achan stole some accursed things, and this resulted in his family being put to death. He introduced the sin of stealing into his family line and all his family suffered retribution, but this time it was almost immediate. They reaped what Achan had sown!

An interesting story concerns a soldier who stole a medal from someone who was dead on the battlefield. It was reported that from that moment on his whole family began to have a problem with pilfering. The tendency to steal actually increased in intensity when the stolen medal was brought into the person's home.

Idolatry

A girl who was adopted by a Christian couple found herself drawn irresistibly towards the occult and into spiritualism. When they investigated the background of the birth mother they found out that she had been involved with many areas of the occult. It was revealed that the mother had used a Ouija board and had attempted suicide after it had spelt out the word 'death' to her. The one area that this girl found most difficult to resist was the use of the Ouija board!

There could of course be a number of reasons why these patterns are repeated. For example, it may simply be that the children are raised in a family atmosphere of drugs or drink, etc., and they are picking up the family patterns. It may be that they are reaping the consequences of living in a dysfunctional family, and they are repeating the dysfunctional behaviour within their own families. There may be physical reasons for repeated patterns or infirmities, or it may be that the children are walking in the path of generational iniquity and are suffering the consequences of their father's sin and thus are following the pattern of 'like father like son.'

It may also, of course, be that a 'familiar spirit' is working through the generational weakness, and is enticing the children into the same sin.

What are Familiar Spirits?

Familiar spirits are demonic beings who will give details about a beloved member of the family who has died. We are expressly forbidden, of course, from seeking after the familiar spirits used in spiritualism. We are also forbidden to ask them questions about the future, etc., as the spiritualist would do.

> *'Give no regard to mediums and familiar spirits; do not seek after them, to be defiled by them: I am the Lord your God.'*
> (Leviticus 19:31)

Isaiah confirms this word and asserts that it is a vain and foolish thing to do:

> *'And when they say to you, "Seek those who are mediums and wizards, who whisper and mutter," should not a people seek their God? Should they seek the dead on behalf of the living?'*
> (Isaiah 8:19)

We are therefore expressly forbidden in Scripture to have anything to do with mediums, or familiar spirits, but sometimes they will attach themselves to a curse which has been put against a family, or to a sin which has been committed. There are a number of ways in which they may obtain an entrance to a family, one of which is through generational sin. They will latch onto the weakness that may have been sown into the family line, and they will seek to seal that weakness in, in order to stay within the familiar setting. They will seek to transfer from one member of the family to another at the moment of death.

The familiar spirit will thus continue down the family line and will actively encourage the weakness, the flaw and the perversity to persist within the generations. Thus the family is not only fighting against the weakness or the tendency to sin in a particular area, but it is also contesting against the familiar spirit. Of course, if a member of the family specific-ally sins by consulting a medium or a familiar spirit, then that would be an open invitation for that familiar spirit to enter the family line and take up residence.

It is very enlightening to see that King Saul consulted a familiar spirit in order to bring Samuel the prophet back from the dead, and also that King Manasseh, that very wicked king of Judah,

> '... made his son pass through the fire, practised soothsaying, used witchcraft, and consulted spiritists and mediums. He did much evil in the sight of the Lord, to provoke Him to anger.'
> (2 Kings 21:6)

As a general rule, when we are ministering into this area of generational iniquity, it is very important to check out whether there are any demonic familiar spirits present, and if so, we need to bind them and cast them out. The person you are praying with will also need to repent on behalf of their ancestors for inviting or allowing them in, and they will need to renounce the work of the enemy as well. We will be considering the subject of how we can be set free from generational iniquity in more depth in a later chapter.

First of all we need to understand how we can discover what damage has been introduced into our family line, and therefore what weaknesses, flaws, tendencies or curses are at work there.

Chapter 10

Discovering Your Family Weaknesses

Before we can receive freedom from generational iniquity we need to know what is at work within **our own** family line, in order that we may take accountability for it and thus bring it before God in confession and repentance. Therefore the question is: 'How can we know what are the sins of our ancestors?' It is very important to realise that some of us will know very little about our family line, especially if we were orphaned or adopted at birth. Maybe, as in the story of one lady, the family had never been a close one and the relatives were kept very much at a distance. In such instances, we can have confidence in the mercy of God, and in a general way confess the sins of our ancestors believing and trusting Him for our cleansing and deliverance.

For those people who do know something about their family background, there are a number of avenues that can be explored. For example, we can look at and **observe** our parents, our grandparents, and even our great-grandparents, to see what is at work within their lives; that is, if such knowledge is available to us. We can **enquire** of those who know something about our family history; it may be that other relatives and friends of the family will be a mine of information. Much can be gleaned from them without entering into any unnecessary gossip.

Another method is to use a '**Family Luggage/Baggage**' sheet (Figure 1), which will help you to see pictorially at a

FAMILY LUGGAGE/BAGGAGE

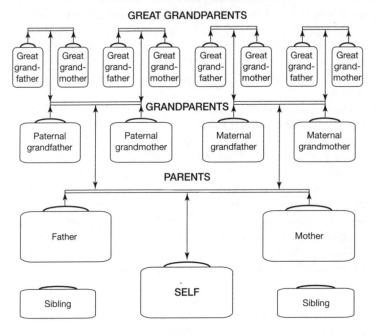

Figure 1

glance the repeating of the patterns, which may be travelling down the family line.

We have already looked at some of these in a previous chapter. but another one, which you may notice, is the pattern of grandmother, mother and daughter, who all dominate and despise their husbands. Ezekiel 16:44–45 is very much up to date:

> *'You are your mother's daughter, loathing husband and children; and you are the sister of your sisters, who loathed their husbands and children.'*

Other patterns, which may become evident, are the various addictive behaviours: alcoholism, drug abuse and adultery being fairly common.

You may also be aware that in your family there is a dabbling in, or a drawing towards false religions: Spiritualism, Freemasonry, or the New Age. In this area it may also be noticeable that confusion, sleepiness, and an enticement towards occultic practices is also apparent, especially when you try to concentrate in worship, read the scriptures or try to pray.

Sometimes it will be seen that there are frequent infirmities travelling down the family line, such illnesses as cancer, abortions, early death, miscarriages, and childlessness to name but a few. We have already seen that this may be as a result of a curse. One lady was convinced that she was the first person in her family ever to have an abortion. To her great surprise, when she shared the truth about the abortion with her mother, she was informed that a number of other women in the family had also had abortions, but everyone had been sworn to secrecy. They remembered that in the history of the family there was often talk concerning a 'gypsy curse'.

Painful emotions can also travel down the family line and these are often linked with the original sin. There may be rejection or a fear of rejection in the family, as happened to one young girl I prayed for. She asked for help because her peers were constantly rejecting her. On inquiring about her family history, she told me that her father had been put out of the house by his grandfather and not allowed to see his family again for many years, because of something which he had done. The father had never forgiven his grandfather and constantly feared more rejection. The fear of rejection had passed down the line from father to daughter and she had inherited and reaped the consequences of further rejection.

One man came to us for prayer because of the deep rage, which would often well up within him, in response to a situation, which was unjust. The rage was totally out of keeping with the circumstances he was facing at the time. On spending some time with him we all were surprised to discover that his grandfather had been involved in a drunken row and in a blind and furious rage had killed a neighbour. That original murder had brought into the family line a tendency towards violence and anger: the sins of the fathers visited upon the children to the third and fourth generation. His father had also suffered violent outbreaks of anger at, and on, inappropriate occasions.

The following are some of the possible sins or weaknesses, which I have personally ministered into on a regular basis and that, are, to some extent fairly common. Fears, phobias, depression, death, grief, disappointment, guilt, false guilt, shame, anxiety, and suicide can all be introduced into the generations either through a particular sin or through a curse and they will continue to have repercussions within the family if they are not dealt with. We have already seen that sexual sin or any kind of abuse (verbal, emotional, physical, and sexual), or sexual perversion, may all be observed to be at work within the family.

Once we have discerned what is at work and where our family weaknesses lie, then we can begin to deal with them, for the good news is that God has already provided the way of escape through the work of the Lord Jesus Christ upon the Cross.

Chapter 11

The Power of the Cross

How do we get free from the generational iniquity within our family line? Thank God that He has already provided a way of escape for us, for Jesus Christ bears our iniquities on the Cross, as well as our sins. In other words He carries the punishment for our own personal sins, as well as the consequences of our ancestor's sin. The Cross is God's answer to the intricate problem of man's sin, his sicknesses, his brokenness, his curses, his griefs, his sorrows, as well as the iniquity which he carries from his ancestors. According to the prophet Isaiah, our iniquity has been borne by Jesus on the Cross:

> *'But He was wounded for our transgressions,*
> *He was bruised for our iniquities;*
> *The chastisement for our peace was upon Him,*
> *And by His stripes we are healed.*
> *All we like sheep have gone astray;*
> *We have turned, every one, to his own way;*
> *And the Lord has laid on Him the iniquity of us all.'*
>
> (Isaiah 53:5–6)

Isn't that a tremendous word of encouragement? There is no condition of man which is not covered by the work of the Lord Jesus Christ upon the Cross.

There is a very interesting picture of the work of Jesus on the Cross, graphically told in Scripture in the book of Leviticus chapter 16, which depicts certain aspects of the atonement. This is the picture of the two goats which were to be presented before God, one of which would be killed and its blood shed for the sins of the people of Israel. It would be a sin offering used for the cleansing of the people; this was to be known as the **sacrificed goat**.

'Then he shall kill the goat of the sin offering, which is for the people, bring its blood inside the veil, do with that blood as he did with the blood of the bull, and sprinkle it on the mercy seat and before the mercy seat. So he shall make atonement for the Holy Place, because of the uncleanness of the children of Israel, and because of their transgressions, for all their sins.' (Leviticus 16:15–16)

In Leviticus 16:21–22 we read of the purpose of the second goat, the life of which was to be retained, but burdened and separated to bear Israel's iniquity. This goat was to be known as the **scapegoat**.

'And Aaron shall lay both his hands on the head of the live goat, confess over it all the iniquities of the children of Israel, and all their transgressions, concerning all their sins, putting them on the head of the goat, and shall send it away into the wilderness by the hand of a suitable man. The goat shall bear on itself all their iniquities to an uninhabited land.'

(Leviticus 16:21–22)

The picture of the two goats gives us a very vivid description of the work of Jesus upon the Cross, for His work is the fulfilment of both the sacrificed goat and the scapegoat. The Cross deals with both the punishment and the consequences of our own sin, and also it is at the Cross where we can be set free from the evil effects of the sins and the iniquities of our ancestors.

Two very important questions would seem to be:
– 'How do we apply the work of Jesus on the Cross to our family sin?'
– 'How can we be released from the sins, the flaw, the weakness and the tendency to sin in our family line and make-up which we have inherited from our ancestors?'

Scripture, fortunately gives us the answer. It is that we find release in the same way in which we found it when we entered into freedom from **our own** personal sin.

First, we need to **recognise** what the iniquities are, and after we do so, we need to take a **responsibility and an accountability** for them as a member of the family line. We then need to stand up and be counted and **confess** and **repent** for the sins of our family, on **behalf** of the family. There is a scriptural precedent for doing this and the promise is that God will hear our **confession and repentance of ancestral sin**:

> *'But if they confess their iniquity and the iniquity of their fathers, with their unfaithfulness in which they were unfaithful to Me, and that they also have walked contrary to Me ... Then I will remember My covenant.'*   (Leviticus 26:40, 42)

Nehemiah repented on behalf of his family line; he recognised and took responsibility for the sin of corruption and the breaking of God's commandments, and he confessed and repented for them before God. Nehemiah chapter 1 records his confession and repentance, not for his own sin, but for the sin of his family and his nation.

> *'We have acted very corruptly against You, and have not kept the commandments, the statues, nor the ordinances which You commanded Your servant Moses.'*   (Nehemiah 1:7)

The leadership of Israel also took responsibility for the nation's generational sin:

> *'Then those of Israelite lineage separated themselves from all foreigners; and they stood and confessed their sins and the iniquities of their fathers.'*   (Nehemiah 9:2)

Ezra also confessed and repented on behalf of his ancestors. We read that he repented of the sin of taking foreign wives and of taking on board their abominations, their idols and false worship. It is very interesting to note that, in actuality, Ezra had not committed these sins personally. He had not taken a foreign wife or worshipped any idols but he was identifying himself with his family's sin, and thus repenting on behalf of his nation and his generational line.

> *'At the evening sacrifice I arose from my fasting; and having torn my garment and my robe, I fell on my knees and spread out my hands to the Lord my God, and said, "Oh my God: I am too ashamed and humiliated to lift up my face to You, my God; for our iniquities have risen higher than our heads, and our guilt has grown up to the heavens. Since the day of our fathers to this day we have been guilty."'* (Ezra 9:5–6)

That is a lovely example of confession and repentance.

As we have seen with the prayer of Ezra and Nehemiah, there is a place for taking accountability for the sins of the ancestors. Just as we personally need to take accountability and responsibility for our own sin, so in the area of generational sin, there comes a time when some member of the family needs to take responsibility for the family sin.

Will God forgive? Will He remove our iniquity from us? Will He deliver us from the weakness, and the flaw in our family line? For encouragement in this, let me refer you to the story of Joshua the high priest.

> *'Then he showed me Joshua the high priest standing before the Angel of the Lord, and Satan standing at his right hand to oppose him.'* (Zechariah 3:1)

The Lord speaks to Satan and rebukes him for his opposition to Joshua, who is evidently clothed in dirty and unkempt garments.

> *'Now Joshua was clothed with filthy garments, and was standing before the Angel. Then He answered and spoke to those who stood before Him, saying, "Take away the filthy garments from him." And to him He said, "See, I have removed your iniquity from you, and I will clothe you with rich robes."'* (Zechariah 3:3–4)

God will forgive. He has provided a way through Jesus to remove our dirty clothes of iniquity from us and He will dress us in His robe of righteousness. In Isaiah chapter 61, we have that lovely encouragement:

> *'I will greatly rejoice in the Lord,*
> *My soul shall be joyful in my God;*
> *For He has clothed me with the garments of salvation,*
> *He has covered me with the robe of righteousness,*
> *As a bridegroom decks himself with ornaments,*
> *And as a bride adorns herself with jewels.'*   (Isaiah 61:10)

So God has promised to set us free from our sins and our iniquities, and as we close the door on our old sinful family line, with all of its weaknesses, so we can ask the Holy Spirit to seal that door with the precious blood of Jesus.

The Good News, however, doesn't end there, for something vital and dynamic was being made available to us through the work of the Lord Jesus Christ upon the Cross; for the work of the Cross is both negative and positive. The negative being that He removes our sin and our generational iniquity from us; through confession and repentance, the door is finally closed and sealed. The positive being that at the Cross we walk through a new door; a door of blessing, a door of new beginnings. For it is at the Cross that Jesus welcomes us into a new family, His family – the **family of God**.

When we are 'born again' through the work of the Holy Spirit, we become part of His family, we become **children of God**, and we inherit all the **blessings** which are His, and which He has won for us through the Cross. He is the second Adam, and as such, His family line is pure and without blemish. He gives to us His robe of righteousness.

The Will of God

On the subject of becoming part of a new family through the Cross, it is vital for us to understand that a mighty work of grace was actually taking place within the confines of the Garden of Gethsemane prior to Jesus' death. Jesus needed to deal with the sin and the stubbornness of the will of mankind. On the night in which Jesus was betrayed, we see Jesus bending the 'will of man' towards the 'will of God'. Three times He cries out to God:

> *'Abba, Father, all things are possible for You. Take this cup away from me; nevertheless, **not what I will, but what You will.**'* (Mark 14:36)

It was in another garden, the Garden of Eden, where the first Adam allowed his will, which originally was bent toward the will of God, to be twisted and bent toward the will of Satan. It was thus in the Garden of Gethsemane that Jesus, at a great cost known only to Himself, bent the 'will of man' back again towards 'the will of God'. With great drops of blood and through enormous stress and distress, He began a new family line which was based on His obedience to the Father, and as we have seen from Deuteronomy chapter 28, obedience brings blessing.

Of course, if that was all that there was available in the Cross it would be wonderful, but we would no doubt, still struggle to obey God's laws ourselves. We understand that Jesus' will was bent towards the will of God, but what about ours? The Scriptures tell us that even that is taken care of. For not only are we 'adopted', 'transferred' into a new family line, we are also given the **'family disposition'**, so that we too can live obedient and blessed lives which will flow through us to our children and to 'our children's children'.

According to Jeremiah the prophet, God says:

> *'I will put My law in their minds, and write it on their hearts; and I will be their God, and they shall be My people ... I will forgive their iniquity, and their sin I will remember no more.'* (Jeremiah 31:33, 34)

The original laws of God were written on stone, but now they are to be written within – on our minds and on our hearts. Thus we will be enabled to 'know' the law of God in our thinking and be able to 'obey' the law from the most inner-most part of our being – even our hearts. However, not only are we given the 'family disposition' we are also given the '**family Spirit**' – the Holy Spirit. The tremendous fact is that God has given to us another promise, a promise that He will put His own Spirit within us, which will enable us and empower us to fulfil His laws from a glad heart.

> *'I will put My Spirit within you and cause you to walk in My statues, and you will keep My judgements and do them.'*
> (Ezekiel 36:27)

Thus we begin to live under the New Covenant, the covenant of blessing through obedience, which is made available to us through the work of the Lord Jesus Christ. The plans and purposes of God will thus be fulfilled, in that He will have a people of His own, who are part of His family, filled with His Spirit, and obedient to His laws. The cry of their hearts will be the same as the cry of Jesus, the Head of the family:

> *'I do not seek My own will but the will of the Father who sent Me.'*
> (John 5:30)

Thus the **law of blessing**, the **law of multiplication** and the **law of sowing and reaping** will be restored to their original purposes, for the desire of God's heart is to always be:

> *'... showing mercy to thousands, to those who love Me and keep My commandments.'*
> (Exodus 20:6)

Appendix

Suggested Prayer of Release from Generational Iniquity

A prayer, confessing the sins of the family and breaking the links:

> 'Father, I thank You that on the Cross You have dealt with all of my sin, through the death and resurrection of the Lord Jesus Christ. Thank You that He paid the penalty for my sins through His shed blood, and that He also carried the punishment for the sins and the iniquities of my ancestors. I thank You too, that according to Your Word, I can come and confess the sins of my forefathers. I do gladly and humbly repent of the sins which my family line have committed back to the third and fourth generation, and to the tenth generation for sexual sin. I especially repent of . . . . *[speak out any specific sins, which you know your family has been into; sexual, addictive, etc.]*.
>
> I also repent of any false worship, which they have given . . . . *[speak out any that are relevant, e.g. Freemasonry, Spiritualism, Buddhism, etc.]*.
>
> I also repent of any occultic activity in my family line . . . . *[speak out any that is known; tarot cards, horoscopes, etc.]*.

Father God, I confess these sins and weaknesses, which may have affected me, and I freely forgive my ancestors in Jesus' Name. I repent and turn away from my own sins in these areas and I renounce Satan and all of his works. I ask You, Heavenly Father, to forgive our sin and to set me, and my family line, free from the consequences of generational iniquity. I ask that the door may be closed and sealed with the precious blood of Jesus.

In His Name I pray. Amen.'